NONFICTION: WRITING FOR FACT AND ARGUMENT

Truthful Biographies

Valerie Bodden

CREATIVE EDUCATION

Published by Creative Education

P.O. Box 227, Mankato, Minnesota 56002

Creative Education is an imprint of The Creative Company

www.thecreativecompany.us

Design and art direction by Rita Marshall

Production by The Design Lab

Printed by Corporate Graphics in the United States of America

Photographs by Alamy (Mary Evans Picture Library), AP Images (Cliff Schiappa), Corbis (Bettmann, Leonard de Selva, Jennifer Kennard, Jeff Spielman), Dreamstime (Rozhenyuk, Moreno Soppelsa), Getty Images (Alfred Eisenstaedt/Time & Life Pictures, E.O. Hoppe/Mansell/Time & Life Pictures, Albert Kaplan), iStockphoto (Don Bayley, Trevor Hunt, Thomas Perkins, Jose Ignacio Soto, John Woodworth)

Excerpt on page 25 adapted from *Act One* by Moss Hart, copyright © 1959 by Catherine Carlisle Hart & Joseph M. Hyman, Trustees. Used by permission of Random House, Inc.

Excerpt on page 32 from *Truman* by David McCullough. Copyright © 1992 by David McCullough. Abridged by permission of Simon & Schuster, Inc.

Library of Congress Cataloging-in-Publication Data

Bodden, Valerie.

Truthful biographies / by Valerie Bodden.

p. cm. — (Nonfiction: writing for fact and argument)

Includes bibliographical references and index.

Summary: An introduction to the ways that writers compose biographies and autobiographies. Excerpts and analysis help to explain the importance of honesty and detail in this nonfiction form.

ISBN 978-1-58341-932-8

1. Biography as a literary form—Juvenile literature. 2. Autobiography—Authorship—Juvenile literature. I. Title.

CT22.B63 2010   809'.93592—dc22   2009024178

CPSIA: 120109 PO1094

First Edition

9 8 7 6 5 4 3 2 1

CONTENTS

When you pick up a story, you expect to be transported into another situation, another person's life, or even another time. If what you hold in your hand is a work of `fiction`, the place to which you will be taken is made up. But, if you happen to be reading a work of `nonfiction`, you will be pulled into a world populated by real people participating in real events—in other words, real life. And real life often proves to be stranger or more relevant than any fictional world could be. Perhaps that's why nonfiction writing so captures the interest of readers around the world who pore over pieces about sports and science, animals and armies, politics, and, perhaps most of all, people.

True stories about real people—biographies—are among the most popular of all nonfiction forms. They allow readers an insider's look at other people's lives, providing insight on famous (or not so famous) individuals and the times in which they lived. Biographies can even help readers to understand themselves better, as readers identify with—or are repulsed by—the books' subjects.

Although writing a biography may seem like a straightforward task—after all, the life has already been lived, and all the author has to do is write it down—it can be surprisingly difficult. Biographers must search out the events of another's life and then shape them into a logical and engaging form. The job is well worth the effort, however, when the subject finally, convincingly, steps off the paper and into the minds of readers.

People have been telling the life stories of others for thousands of years. The first biographies were not written down but were passed from one generation to another through oral poems and songs. Written biographies first began to flourish in ancient Greece and Rome during the early centuries A.D., penned by writers such as Plutarch, Suetonius, and Tacitus. These writers grappled with the questions of how much of their writing should focus on the accomplishments of the great figures they portrayed (biography then was focused exclusively on people of achievement, such as Julius Caesar or Alexander the Great, rather than ordinary folk), and how much they should reveal of their subject's faults and failings. In this, these writers had something in common with biographers through the ages.

For a time after the fall of the Western Roman Empire in the fifth century A.D., written biography was all but given up. Those life stories that did make it onto paper were hagiographies (*hay-gee-AH-gruh-feez*), which focused on the lives of saints and offered only positive portraits of their subjects. During the Renaissance of the

14th through 16th centuries, the genre experienced a rebirth along with other art forms. Renewed focus on ancient Greek and Roman works led writers to choose secular subjects and also revived the tension between writing biographies as a way of applauding achievement and writing them to depict real people with all their flaws.

In the 18th century, English author Samuel Johnson revolutionized biography, writing that if an author "professes to write *A Life*, he must represent it really as it was." Regarded as the father of modern biography, Johnson encouraged writers to portray not only their subject's public life and accomplishments but his or her inner workings and private affairs. Furthermore, to Johnson's mind, famous individuals were not the only proper subjects for biography.

Johnson's beliefs spurred a generation of writers to pen works that divulged both their subjects' virtues and their failures. By the Victorian Age of the 19th century, however, biographers had largely turned from Johnson's ways and were again focusing only on their subjects' public achievements. These hagiographies

almost always portrayed important men (not women), with the purpose of providing an example or lesson to readers. According to English author H. G. Wells, who lived to see the end of the Victorian Age, Victorian biographies were "unsatisfactory" and "untruthful," telling "the worst kind of falsehood—the falsehood of omission."

Fortunately for Wells, a new biographer was about to enter the literary scene—one who didn't believe in glossing over a person's imperfections. In 1918, English biographer Lytton Strachey published *Eminent Victorians*, a chronicle of four famous figures who had long been hailed as heroes. His witty, mocking portraits helped to change the purpose of biography from commemoration to truthful representation of a subject. See if you can figure out why as you read the following selection from *Eminent Victorians*, in which Strachey portrays the founder of modern nursing, Florence Nightingale, as she works at a hospital for wounded soldiers during the Crimean War (1853–56).

Biographer Lytton Strachey
(1880–1932)

Wherever, in those vast wards, suffering was at its worst and the need for help was greatest, there, as if by magic, was Miss Nightingale. . . . Over and over again her untiring efforts rescued those whom the surgeons had abandoned as beyond the possibility of cure. . . .

Certainly, she was heroic. Yet her heroism was not of that simple sort so dear to the readers of novels and the compilers of hagiologies—the romantic sentimental heroism with which mankind loves to invest its chosen darlings: it was made of sterner stuff. . . . It was not by gentle sweetness . . . that she had brought order out of chaos in the Scutari hospitals. . .; it was by strict method, by stern discipline, by rigid attention to detail, by ceaseless labor, by the fixed determination of an indomitable [unconquerable] *will. Beneath her cool and calm demeanor lurked fierce and passionate fires. As she passed through the wards in her plain dress, so quiet, so unassuming, she struck the casual observer simply as the pattern of a perfect lady; but the keener eye perceived something more than that—the serenity of high deliberation in the scope of the capacious* [large] *brow, the sign of power in the dominating curve of the thin nose, and the traces of a harsh and dangerous temper—something peevish, something mocking, and yet something precise—in the small and delicate mouth. . . . As for her voice, . . . those clear tones were in no need of emphasis: "I never heard her raise her voice," said one of her companions. Only, when she had spoken, it seemed as if nothing could follow but obedience. . . .*

[In letters,] . . . her pen . . . would rush on to the discussion of individuals, to the denunciation of an incompetent surgeon or the ridicule of a self-sufficient nurse. Her sarcasm searched the ranks of the officials with the deadly and unsparing precision of a machine-gun. Her nicknames [for others] were terrible.

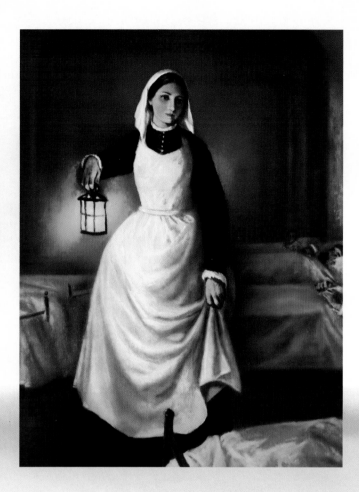

Before this time, according to Strachey, Florence Nightingale had been pictured as a "saintly, self-sacrificing woman, the delicate maiden of high degree." Strachey tears down this image. Although he acknowledges Nightingale's heroism and shows us her heroic acts, he does not do so at the expense of revealing her temper and coldness. Indeed, he makes it apparent

An artistic rendering of Florence Nightingale

that some of these very character traits enabled her to bring about the needed reform in military hospitals. Strachey's determination to exclude "everything that is redundant and nothing that is significant" influenced the biographers who would come after him, and life stories revealing the personality—warts and all—of their subjects grew in popularity.

By the time World War II had ended in 1945, biographies had reached a new level of prominence, and that popularity has only continued to grow in the half century since. Today, most biographers still share Strachey's belief that although shortcomings can make a subject less noble, they can also make him or her more human—and we can all relate to that!

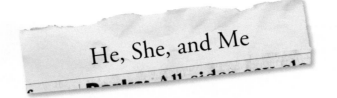

He, She, and Me

The word "biography" comes from the Greek words for "life" and "writing." In general, biographies are written by one person about the life of one other person (although the people who play important roles in the subject's life also appear in the story). Some biographies, however, depict the lives of more than one subject, focusing perhaps on a family or a group of people who were involved in an important event together. Such multiple biographies are among the most difficult to write because the author must make clear the interactions between the subjects and the influences they have on one another.

Whether about single or multiple subjects, biographies are generally written in the `third person` point of view (using "he" or "she"). That does not mean that you cannot write your own life story, however. After all, who knows more about your life than you do? A true life story written *by* you *about* you is called an autobiography or memoir. Although both autobiographies and memoirs are written in the `first person` (using "I"), autobiographies generally cover the whole scope of a person's life, while memoirs focus on one period

15

or aspect of that life. Both memoirs and autobiographies allow writers to explore their lives and try to make sense of their experiences.

As readers, we may gravitate to memoirs and autobiographies because they bring us into the private thoughts of another human being and allow us to hear her unique voice as she tells her own story. They can also carry us into an era long gone or a part of the world we have never seen, allowing us to experience it as the writer did. As we read, however, we must keep in mind that autobiographers and memoirists can select which scenes from their life to include. Although some writers may be painfully honest, others may choose to leave out the scene where they bullied a younger kid, for example, in order to shine a better light on their

lives. In some cases, memoirists have even been
accused of making up entire scenes of their life,
just to make their story more compelling. Even
when writers are completely honest about their
lives, we have to remember that they are describing events from their own unique perspective,
which may not be how the other people involved in
their life viewed the same events.

In the following excerpt from American author
Mark Twain's memoir *Life on the Mississippi* (1883),
about his experiences as a steamboat pilot on the
Mississippi River, take note of the author's unique
voice, as well as his perspective on his experiences. Do you get the sense he is painting an
honest picture of his life?

I entered upon the small enterprise of "learning" twelve or thirteen hundred miles of the great Mississippi River with the easy confidence of my time of life. If I had really known what I was about to require of my faculties, I should not have had the courage to begin. I supposed that all a pilot had to do was to keep his boat in the river, and I did not consider that that could be much of a trick, since it was so wide.

The boat backed out from New Orleans at four in the afternoon, and it was "our watch" until eight. Mr. Bixby, my chief, "straightened her up," plowed her along past the sterns of the other boats that lay at the Levee, and then said, "Here, take her; shave those steamships as close as you'd peel an apple." I took the wheel, and my heartbeat fluttered up into the hundreds; for it seemed to me that we were about to scrape the side off every ship in the line, we were so close. I held my breath and began to claw the boat away from the danger; and I had my own opinion of the pilot who had known no better than to get us into such peril, but I was too wise to express it…. Within ten seconds more I was set aside in disgrace, and Mr. Bixby was going into danger again and flaying me alive with abuse of my cowardice. I was stung, but I was obliged to admire the easy confidence with which my chief loafed from side to side of his wheel, and trimmed the ships so closely that disaster seemed ceaselessly imminent….

Now and then Mr. Bixby called my attention to certain things. Said he, "This is Six-Mile Point." I assented. It was pleasant enough information, but I could not see the bearing of it.

As you read this selection, could you picture
Mark Twain (whose birth name was Samuel Clemens)
as a young man at the wheel of a steamboat? The
author's youthful enthusiasm is apparent in
his eagerness to set out on his adventure, with
no idea of the challenges it will bring. Twain
doesn't hide the fact that he was a naïve youth
when he first set out on the Mississippi. Writing

Author Mark Twain (1835-1910)
upon the deck of a steamboat

In accordance with the Act of Congress, approved Aug. 30, 1852.

The Original Renewed.

No. 596

PILOT'S CERTIFICATE.

The undersigned, Inspectors for the District of St. Louis, certify that *Samuel Clemens* having been by them this day duly examined, touching his qualifications as a **Pilot** of a Steam Boat, is a suitable and safe person to be intrusted with the power and duties of Pilot of Steam Boats, and do license him to act as such for one year from this date, on the following rivers, to wit: *the St. Mississippi River to and from St. Louis and New Orleans*

Given under our hands, this 9th day of April 1859.

James H. M'Cord

McLunglelon

I, *James H. M'Cord*, Inspector for the District of St. Louis, certify that the above named *Sam'l Clemens* this day, before me, solemnly swore that he would faithfully and honestly, according to his best skill and judgment, without concealment or reservation, perform all the duties required of him as a Pilot, by the Act of Congress, approved August 30, 1852, entitled "An act to amend an act entitled An act to provide for the better security of the lives of passengers on board of vessels propelled in whole or in part by steam; and for other purposes."

the book from his older—and wiser—perspective,
he knows now what he didn't know then: that pilot-
ing the Mississippi would be hard work, and that
he had no idea how to do it. In fact, he didn't
even know that there was anything he needed to
learn. When Mr. Bixby tried to teach him about the
various points on the river, he "did not see the
bearing of it."

In addition to giving us a feel for the author
and his attitudes, this selection also brings
us back to a time when steamboats ruled the
Mississippi, carrying people and goods from one
part of the nation to another. We can picture
Twain's steamboat scraping close to the sides of
the vessels that crowd the river and are reminded
of how different Twain's time was from ours. Yet,
our time can make for interesting reading, too—not
only to future readers but also to those of today.
So sit down and write about your world, your
thoughts, your experiences—who knows what others
may learn from your autobiography or memoir!

Mark Twain's steamboat
pilot's license

The first step in writing any biography, of course, is deciding *who* it will be about. Yourself? Your mother? A celebrity? The president? A historical figure? All of these people could be legitimate subjects for a biography, as long as you are interested enough in them to spend the time needed to learn about their lives. And you definitely will need to spend time learning about that life before you can write about it. Research may sound like the boring part of writing a biography, but it doesn't have to be. Think of yourself as a detective, searching out every last clue about a person's life so that you can solve the mystery of who he really is.

Whenever possible, research should involve a combination of primary and secondary sources. Primary sources give you the subject's thoughts directly, through diaries, letters, interviews, or speeches. Secondary sources, such as newspapers and other biographies about the subject, tell you what other people have said about this person. As you research, remember that it's important to get your facts right, so check and double-check them. After all, people who read your biography will form an opinion of the subject based upon what you say about him.

After you've completed your research, you must decide which pieces of a person's life you will put into your biography. You'll want to give a fair and balanced account of your subject, but you cannot possibly include everything that ever happened to him. You will need to figure out what the reader needs to know in order to understand your subject. For example, maybe he broke his leg at the age of 12. If this led him to quit sports and pursue writing, you would probably want to include it. If, on the other hand, it had little effect on the overall course of his life, you might consider leaving it out of your biography.

Once you are ready to begin writing your biography, you may think that the task will be simple—start with the subject's birth and stop with his death. This is certainly one way of relating a biography, but it is not the only way. Some authors choose to introduce a biography with an important event from the subject's life, no matter how old he was when it occurred, before going back and relating the rest of the biography in chronological order. Other biographers choose not to follow a chronology at all, but instead cover their subject's life topically. If the subject is an actor,

THEATRE MAGAZINE
35 CENTS · NOVEMBER 1925

for example, sections may be focused on movies in which he has starred.

In the following introduction from American playwright and theater director Moss Hart's *Act One: An Autobiography* (1959), notice how the author begins his life story with an important moment from his childhood.

A 1925 issue of *Theatre Magazine*

That afternoon, I went to work at the music store as usual. It was just around the corner from where we lived, and I worked there every afternoon from three o'clock until seven, while its owner, a violin and piano teacher on the side, gave the lessons which more or less supported the store.... The sparseness of the customers ... allowed me to finish my homework as rapidly as possible and then pore greedily over as many copies of Theatre Magazine *as the library would allow me to take out at one time.*

It was, as far as I was concerned, the perfect job. There was usually even enough time, before Mr. Levenson returned at seven o'clock, for a good half-hour or so of pure, idle dreaming; a necessity as basic to a twelve-year-old boy as food and drink....

This afternoon, ... as I entered the store, and before I could even toss my books and magazines on the counter, Mr. Levenson was speaking....

"Do you think," he said, while I was still in the doorway, "your mother would let you go downtown alone, just this once? I need some music for tomorrow's lessons...."

I can still recall my excitement as the subway doors opened at Times Square, and I shall certainly never forget the picture that greeted me as I dashed up the stairs and stood gaping at my first sight of Broadway and 42nd Street. A swirling mob of happy, laughing people filled the streets, and others hung from the windows of nearly every building....

In that first breathless look it seemed completely right somehow that the glittering Broadway of my fantasy should be as dazzling as this even in broad daylight, but what I took to be an everyday occurrence was Broadway waiting to celebrate the election of ... the next President of the United States.

With this introduction of a life-changing moment from his boyhood, Hart pulls us into his life, making us want to read more about why this moment was so important to him and what influence it would have on him as he grew up. That is the goal of any good introduction—to intrigue readers and leave us wanting more. Hart's introduction also foreshadows his future, which will be wrapped up in "glittering Broadway" as he works his way up from office boy and actor to become an award-winning playwright and director. In the chapter following the introduction, Hart goes on to relate the story of his birth, childhood, and ancestry, and the rest of the book tells of his adventures in the theater in a fairly straightforward chronological order.

Hart does not end his book with his death, however (indeed, no autobiographer can), but stops after his first great success on Broadway, the play *Once in a Lifetime* (1930). Like autobiographies, biographies don't always end with their subject's death. Some stop well before it, while others carry on past the subject's death, showing how he has left a lasting mark on the world.

So play with the order of your biography, putting
your subject's birth here and his death there—or
his death here and his birth there—until everything has fallen into just the right place to tell
his story as only you can tell it.

Playwright Moss Hart
(1904-61) in Times Square

THE WHITE HOUSE
WASHINGTON

Dear Bess:— Well

letter organized now

farm sale

t store,

Margie

HEADQUARTERS
NDRED TWENTY NINTH
ELD ARTILLERY

Miss Bess Wallace
219 Delaware St
Ind

es Senate
nstate commerce
EE   AiR Mail

WASHINGTON
AUG 5
7-PM
M 1942

Mr. Harry S Truman
219 North Delaware St.
Independence, Mo.

United States S
SPECIAL COMMITTEE INVESTIGA
THE NATIONAL DEFENSE PR

As a biographer, you don't have to create characters as you would in fiction. The characters
already exist. But it is your job to bring them
to life on the page. Readers want to know what
your subject looked like, what she sounded like,
what she ate, and more. And they don't want only
to know about her good side; don't forget to
include information on her relevant failings and
mistakes. (Of course, your goal should not be to
`defame` her character, but simply to show that
she is, after all, only human.) The main subject
of a biography should obviously receive the lion's
share of attention, but don't neglect to describe
the other people who come into that person's life
as well.

One of the best ways to bring a person to life
on the page is to include things she said or wrote.
Quotes, which can come from diaries, letters,
autobiographies, or interviews, help readers hear
the subject's voice and get a feel for her personality. Some biographers write quotes from letters
or diaries as if they are dialogue with another
person rather than written correspondence. Other
authors, however, insist on providing quotes in

Mailed correspondence of
U.S. president Harry Truman

29

their proper `context` and citing them as part of a written work. Either method can be acceptable, depending on the intended audience or publisher.

In addition to seeing your subject come alive on the page, readers want to see the world in which that person lives. Where was she born? At what time in history? Especially for biographies about historical figures, you cannot assume that readers already know all there is to know about the time period in which the subject lived. And often, the details of that time period are key to understanding your subject's actions and thoughts. Historical details can also help readers see a person's life in the context of what was happening in the wider world. In some cases, you will also want to include background information on your subject's profession or field of study. A biography on Polish scientist Marie Curie, for example, might need to include information on radioactivity. Descriptions of such background information should usually be sprinkled throughout a work in order to avoid overwhelming the reader—or bogging the biography down—with one long history, geography, or science lesson.

The following excerpt from the biography *Truman* (1992) by American author David McCullough uses quotes and background information about the American frontier to bring to life the story of the 33rd U.S. president Harry Truman's grandparents, Anderson and Mary Jane Truman, who settled in Missouri in 1846. As you read, try to pick out the details about each of these subjects and the world in which they lived.

A portrait of Harry Truman

Andy, as [Anderson] was called, grew up on the Truman farm near the tiny crossroads village of Christianburg, Kentucky. He was slight, gentle, soft-spoken, thirty years old, and without prospects. Nonetheless, Mary Jane Holmes, who was five years younger, had seen enough in him to defy her mother and marry him....

The wedding took place in Kentucky in mid-August at the home of the married sister, a handsome red-brick house with white trim that still stands. Then Mary Jane's "Mr. Truman," as she would always refer to him, set off by horse for "the wild country" of Missouri, intending to stay only long enough to secure the blessing of his new mother-in-law.

His first letter from Missouri reached Mary Jane a month later. To his amazement, he had been welcomed with open arms, her mother and sisters all hugging and kissing him, everybody laughing and crying at once. He was urged to stay and take up the frontier life. He could be happy anywhere, even in Missouri, he wrote to Mary Jane, if only she were with him. "As for myself I believed that I would be satisfied if you was out here.... I believe I can live here if you are willing."

She arrived by steamboat, and with her mother's blessing and the wedding gift of a ... slave named Hannah and her child, the young couple settled on a rented farm belonging to a prominent local figure....

Independence, "Queen City of the Trails," was the country's first western boomtown, and to newly arrived settlers, after long days on the river, it seemed a metropolis of stores, blacksmith sheds, wagon shops, of crowded streets and unceasing commotion. The crack of bullwhips split the air like rifle fire as wagon trains made up for Oregon.

Did Anderson and Mary Jane jump off the page
at you as you read this selection? That's because
McCullough has skillfully woven details about each
person into his biography. Anderson is described
as "slight, gentle," and it is obvious that the
two love each other deeply. Mary Jane respects her
husband so much that she calls him "Mr. Truman"

Late-19th-century arrivals
to St. Louis, Missouri

even after they are married, and he adores her
so much that he can be happy anywhere, as long as
she is there, too. Notice how McCullough doesn't
just tell us that Anderson can be happy anywhere;
he also lets us hear it from Anderson himself,
through a quote from a letter he sent Mary Jane.
That quote not only gives us evidence that what
McCullough is telling us is true; it also helps us
to hear Anderson's unique, "soft-spoken" style.

It's not only Anderson and Mary Jane that we
can picture after reading this excerpt, though.
We can also see the times and town in which they
live. We see that they were married before slavery
was outlawed, as the couple is given a slave as
a wedding gift. McCullough also introduces us to
the frontier town of Independence, with its chaos,
crowds, and cracking bullwhips. Notice that he has
incorporated powerful sensory descriptions into
this scene, helping us to feel almost as if we are
there with Anderson and Mary Jane Truman. So sit
down and let your words sketch out the world in
which your characters live—then sketch the characters in, too—and invite readers to step into
your word painting.

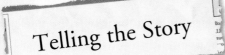

Telling the Story

Think of the most exciting fictional tales you've
ever read. They probably caught and held your
attention by telling stories. Although a biography
is not made up, it *is* a story—a life story. And,
in order to draw and hold your reader's attention,
you will probably want to tell it like a story.
Simply listing all the facts you've learned about
your subject's life may be informative, but it
will likely also be dull. You want to weave these
facts into a `narrative` that is not only truthful
but also compelling and that makes readers feel as
if they are watching these events unfold—again!

Many biographers draw on techniques from fiction writing in order to make their biographies
come to life. This is fine—as long as you are
sticking to the facts, you can relate your biography in any way that seems exciting to you. Many
biographies are told as a series of connected
scenes from the subject's life. Others create
suspense by foreshadowing what is to come in later
scenes or by writing "cliffhangers" to end scenes.

Beginning fiction writers are often given
the advice, "Show, don't tell," but that advice
applies to biography writers as well. If you can

show your subject doing something that reveals his personality, it will be much more powerful than if you simply *tell* us that he had a specific trait. For example, if your subject was notoriously cheap, don't tell us he was cheap; show him, for example, taking his future wife on their first date—and expecting her to pay for dinner. This allows us not only to see his personality but also to make our own judgments about it.

As you reveal the various scenes of your subject's life, you will likely spend more time on some portions than on others. You may choose to gloss over relatively unimportant periods in a sentence or two, while you may devote a half-dozen paragraphs or more to a single life-changing day. No matter how much time you spend on a particular period, however, it's a good idea to let the reader know the date from time to time in order to avoid confusion.

Sometimes, you may come upon periods in your subject's life for which little information is available. You may choose to ignore these periods, simply writing that it is unknown what your subject did during this time. Some biographers use this as an opportunity to speculate (based on what they *do* know) on what might have happened. Other authors even speculate (again based on the facts available) on what their subject is thinking at certain times. For example, in *The Life of Abraham Lincoln* (1900), American author Ida Tarbell writes of the Lincoln family's move from Kentucky to Indiana: "To a boy of seven years, free from all responsibility, and too vigorous to feel its hardships, such a journey must have been a long delight and wonder." Tarbell doesn't know exactly how the young Lincoln felt, but based on the facts, she can make an educated guess on what the journey "must have" been like for him.

Tarbell creates a number of vivid narratives in her work on Lincoln, including the following, about the night he was assassinated. Notice how she relates this incident not as a series of facts but as a compelling story, showing us exactly what happened.

When the presidential party finally entered the theater, making its way along the gallery behind the seats of the dress circle, the orchestra broke into "Hail to the Chief," and the people, rising in their seats and waving hats and handkerchiefs, cheered and cheered, the actors on the stage standing silent in the meantime. The party passed through the narrow entrance into the box, and the several members laid aside their wraps [coats], and bowing and smiling to the enthusiastic crowd below, seated themselves, Mr. Lincoln in a large armchair at the left, Mrs. Lincoln next to him...; and then the play went on.

The party in the box was well entertained, it seemed, especially the President, who laughed good-humoredly at the jokes and chatted cheerfully between the acts. He moved from his seat but once, rising then to put on his overcoat, for the house was chilly. The audience was well entertained, too, though not a few kept an eye on the box entrance, still expecting General Grant. The few whose eyes sought the box now and then noticed, in the second scene of the third act, that a man was passing behind the seats of the dress circle and approaching the entrance to the box....

Opening the door so quietly that no one heard him, the man entered the box. Then if any eye in the house could but have looked, if one head in the box had been turned, it would have been seen that the man held in his right hand a Derringer pistol, and that he raised the weapon and aimed it steadily at the head of the smiling President.

No eye saw him, but a second later and every ear heard a pistol shot.

THE ASSASSINATION OF PRESIDENT LINCOLN AT FORD'S THEATRE ON THE NIGHT OF APRIL 14, 1865.

The moment of President
Lincoln's assassination

With this powerful account, Tarbell makes us
feel as if we are in the theater with the president
when he is shot. We experience the excitement of
the crowd at the president's entrance, feel the
suspense (since we know the fateful outcome) of
the man opening the door to the president's box,
and hear the report of the pistol shot. Tarbell
takes her time describing this all-important
scene, despite the fact that it took place over the
course of only a single evening.

As Tarbell's writing demonstrates, the key to
turning a life into an exciting story is to show
it as it actually happened. No matter whose life
you choose to write about, you can do that, too.
So search out the facts and details, arrange them
into a logical order, and then piece them together
to create a person—one who actually lived and
breathed and who will live and breathe anew on the
pages of your biography!

A portrait of Abraham
Lincoln at age 33

Digging up the Evidence

Some people have left behind volumes and volumes
of letters and diaries, while others have barely
recorded a written word. Either way, it is your job
as a biographer to find as much information as you
can on your subject. First, think of a person you
have always wanted to know more about. One of the
first places to look for clues to your subject's
life is in books, so take a trip to the library to
see how many are available on him or her. While
you're there, ask the librarian to show you how to
look up old newspaper and magazine articles. These
can provide accounts of your subject from his or
her contemporaries. As you research, take notes
on your findings, and when you are done, write a
paragraph that summarizes your subject's life.
Don't forget to include his or her mistakes along
with the achievements.

Practicing the Interview

Although interviews involve simply talking with
another person, they can be nerve-wracking. In
order to get comfortable with conducting interviews, it can help to practice. Choose another
person who interests you—this one living and
accessible (perhaps a relative, friend, or
teacher)—and who is willing to be interviewed.
Think carefully about which questions you want to
ask the person, and write them down. Then, interview away. Take notes on the person's answers,
and if you think of more questions while you're
talking, feel free to ask them. Try to find out
not only what has happened in your subject's life,
but also how it has affected him or her. After
the interview, look over your notes. Do you have
enough information to write a short biography of
this person? If so, write it! If not, go back and
ask more questions until you do.

Write Your Life

In theory, the easiest life story to write should
be our own. After all, we've lived it, and no one
knows our memories or thoughts better. Writing an
autobiography isn't necessarily easy, however.
In order to get started, it can be helpful to
create a timeline. First, make a list of all the
years in your life. Beside each year, write down
any major events that you remember. For example:
"1997—born." For events from your earliest childhood, it might help to look at pictures or talk to
your parents. Now try to fill in information about
each of these events more fully. Where were you
born? What was the weather like that day? Did anything unusual happen? When you are done, look over
your timeline. Are there any events that could be
eliminated from your autobiography without affect-
ing its overall course? Highlight the five most
important events in your life—the ones that have
helped to shape you.

Telling the Story

Sometimes, the best way to get someone interested
in a life story is to begin by telling a story. Look
back at the timeline of your life. What one event
might make a compelling story? Your birth? A family vacation? Failing a test? Write about it! Don't
just tell readers what happened, though; show them.
Aim to create a scene that makes readers feel as if
they are there with you. What did you see and hear?
Was there a particular smell in the air? Who else
was there? What were you doing? When you are done,
have a family member or friend read your introduction. If it leads them to want to read more about
your life, you've done your job. If not, go back and
`revise` your narrative until you have a compelling story that draws readers into your life.

LOSSARY

chronological following the order of time; something that is related chronologically tells what happened first, then what happened next, and so on

contemporaries people who lived at or around the same time as another person

context the circumstances that surround something (or someone) and within which it exists

defame to hurt someone's reputation through false and damaging statements

fiction literary works in which situations, characters, and events are made up; novels and short stories are works of fiction

first person a perspective, pronoun, or verb form that refers to the speaker or writer; in English, "I" and "we" are first-person pronouns

hagiographies biographies about saints or that idealize or worship their subjects

naïve simple and lacking experience or understanding

narrative a story, as opposed to exposition (which generally provides background information)

nonfiction writing that is based on facts rather than fiction

perspective the position from which a person views people, objects, or events; how a person sees the world

Renaissance the time in European history, from the 14th through 16th centuries, that was marked by a renewal of classical art and literature and the beginnings of modern science and exploration

revise to rewrite for the purpose of improving

secular describing matters that are worldly or physi-
cal as opposed to spiritual or religious

third person a perspective, pronoun, or verb form
that refers to someone or something being spoken about;
in English, third-person pronouns include "he," "she,"
"it," and "they"

Victorian Age the time period, from 1837 to 1901,
during which Queen Victoria reigned in England; attitudes at the time were generally stiff and conventional

SELECTED ⒷIBLIOGRAPHY

Bowen, Catherine Drinker. *Biography: The Craft and the
Calling*. Boston: Little, Brown and Company, 1969.

Hamilton, Nigel. *Biography: A Brief History*. Cambridge,
Mass.: Harvard University Press, 2007.

———. *How to Do Biography: A Primer*. Cambridge, Mass.:
Harvard University Press, 2008.

Hampl, Patricia, and Elaine Tyler May, eds. *Tell Me
True: Memoir, History, and Writing a Life*. St. Paul:
Borealis Books, 2008.

Taylor, Ina. *Writing Biographies and Getting Published*.
Lincolnwood, Ill.: NTC/Contemporary Publishing, 1999.

Zinsser, William. *On Writing Well: The Classic Guide to
Writing Nonfiction*. New York: HarperCollins, 1994.

NDEX